尾田栄一郎

Here's volume 10. It's been two years since I started this series. Two years...two years... Back then Sazae-san, who's 24, was only 24... Oh, now that I think about it, I'm now the same age as Sazae-san. But it seems like I used to be the same age as Katsuo-kun. Who will it be next? Norisuke-kun? Taiko-san? Tara-san? It makes me laugh to say "Tara-san." Or "Ikura-san." What am I going on about? Anyway, I'm the same as ever—not working, just drawing manga.

-Eiichiro Oda, 1999

Editor's note: The aforementioned names belong to ageless characters from the beloved cartoon series, *Sazae-san*.

Eiichiro Oda began his manga career at the age of 17, when his one-shot cowboy manga **Wanted!** won second place in the coveted Tezuka manga awards. Oda went on to work as an assistant to some of the biggest manga artists in the industry, including Nobuhiro Watsuki, before winning the Hop Step Award for new artists. His pirate adventure **One Piece**, which debuted in **Weekly Shonen Jump** in 1997, quickly became one of the most popular manga in Japan.

ONE PIECE VOL. 10
EAST BLUE PART 10

SHONEN JUMP Manga Edition

This volume contains material that was originally
published in English in **SHONEN JUMP** #36–38.

STORY AND ART BY EIICHIRO ODA

English Adaptation/Lance Caselman
Translation/Naoko Amemiya
Touch-up Art & Lettering/Mark McMurray
Additional Touch-up/Josh Simpson
Design/Sean Lee
Editor/Yuki Takagaki

Printed in Italy

Published by VIZ Media, LLC
P.O. Box 77010
San Francisco, CA 94107

25
First printing, April 2006
Twenty-fifth printing, July 2024

viz.com

ONE PIECE

#10

"OK, Let's Stand Up!"

STORY AND ART BY **EIICHIRO ODA**

Genzo

Nojiko

"Red-Haired" Shanks

THE STORY OF ONE PIECE
Volume 10

Monkey D. Luffy started out as just a kid with a dream — and that dream was to become the greatest pirate in history! Stirred by the tales of pirate "Red-Haired" Shanks, Luffy vowed to become a pirate himself. That was before the enchanted Devil Fruit gave Luffy the power to stretch like rubber, at the cost of being unable to swim — a serious handicap for an aspiring sea dog. Undeterred, Luffy set out to sea and recruited some crewmates: lying sharpshooter Usopp, master swordsman Zolo, and treasure-hunting thief Nami.

Luffy and his shipmates have finally defeated Don Krieg and his pirates and added the high-kicking cook Sanji to their crew. At last it seems they can finally set sail for the Grand Line—until they discover that their navigator, Nami, has deserted! Zolo and Usopp sail after her and come upon an island under the tyrannical rule of the fiendish Fish-Man Pirates and their leader, Captain "Saw-Tooth" Arlong. Worse still, Nami is in cahoots with them.

Luffy and the others reach the island, but despite what they hear about Nami they refuse to believe it. They come to understand Nami's hatred of pirates when they learn from her foster sister, Nojiko, that their adoptive mother, Belle-Mère, was killed by Arlong. They discover, too, that Nami has been hoarding her loot to buy Coco Village back from Arlong. Nami, who has been fighting a solitary battle for so long, finally asks Luffy for help.

Kuroobi

Sanji
The kind-hearted cook (and ladies' man) whose dream is to find the legendary sea, the "All Blue."

Hatchan (Hachi)

Nami
A thief who specializes in robbing pirates. Nami hates pirates, but Luffy convinced her to join his crew as navigator.

Monkey D. Luffy
Boundlessly optimistic and able to stretch like rubber, he is determined to become the King of the Pirates.

Roronoa Zolo
A former bounty hunter and master of the "three-sword" fighting style. He plans to become the world's greatest swordsman!

Arlong

Usopp
A village boy with a talent for telling tall tales. His father, Yasopp, is a member of Shanks's crew.

Choo

Vol. 10
OK, Let's STAND UP!

CONTENTS

EIICHIRO ODA

ONE PIECE

1 STAND BY

2 STAND BY

3 STAND THE PAIN

5 STAND BY

4 STAND BY

EPISODE 82 "OK, Let's STAND UP!"

8

YOU'D BETTER STOP...

SWUP

FIRST YOU GOTTA TELL US YOUR STORY.

AYE...

HEH HEH HEH. STOP RIGHT THERE.

WHERE DO YOU THINK YOU'RE GOING?

SHFF

SHFF SHFF

KR

OUTTA MY WAY.

!!?

!!!

WHAT BUSINESS DO YOU HAVE WITH ME, PIRATE?

SHFF SHFF SHFF...

KERPLONK

HEY !!

!

HOW GENEROUS OF YOU, USOPP...

I-IT'S OKAY WITH ME IF YOU DON'T SHARE, LUFFY.

JUST SAVE A LITTLE FOR THE REST OF US.

OKAY.

krak krak

PIRATES, EH? SO THAT'S THE CONNECTION.

LONG NOSE IS ALIVE!!

I THOUGHT NAMI KILLED HIM!!

THAT'S THE GUY THAT TRICKED ME!!

RORONOA ZOLO!!

HE TOOK ME FOR A RIDE... I MEAN, I TOOK HIM FOR A RIDE!!

14

HA HA HA HA!! YOU'RE JUST FOUR PEOPLE FROM AN INFERIOR SPECIES.

WHAT CAN YOU DO!!?

YOU MEAN TO TELL ME...

...YOU CAME HERE FOR NAMI?

NO!!!

WHAT?

TOOT-TOOT-TOOOOT-TOOT-TOOOT?

ARISE, GIANT WARRIOR!!!

DO YOU BONEHEADS THINK...

...YOU CAN PUSH LORD ARLONG AROUND? I'LL TURN YOU INTO CHUM!!!

OOOOO

THE MONSTER FROM THE GRAND LINE!!

AGH! WHAT IS IT!!?

AAAAAH

THE ONE THAT DECI-MATED GOSA!!

OH, IT'S JUST HIM.

SO HE WORKS FOR THESE GUYS.

WHERE ARE YOU GOING !!?

WAIT, MOMOO !!

SWOO ..... SH

MOO ...

MOO-HOO !!!

WHAT DO YOU THINK YOU'RE DOING?

MOMOO ?

...I WON'T STOP YOU.

WELL, IF YOU WANT TO RUN AWAY...

SH AK E!!

shake shake shake shake

GO AHEAD, MOMOO.

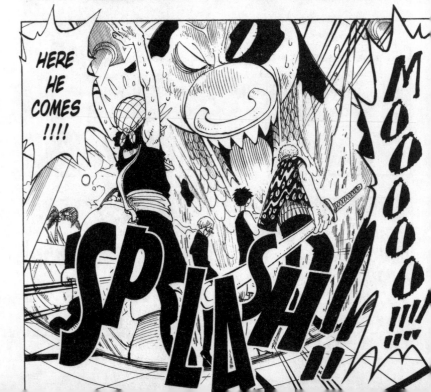

HERE HE COMES !!!!

MOOOOO!!!!

SPLASH!!!

I WAS JUST THINKING ABOUT CLOBBERING YOU, TOO.

WELL THAT WORKS OUT PERFECTLY.

SMEK. ♡

I'LL SHOW YOU THAT HUMANS ARE NO MATCH FOR FISHMEN!

WHAT HE DID TO OUR COMRADES WASN'T NICE!!!

LOOKS LIKE WE'LL HAVE TO GET INVOLVED.

DO-DO-OM!!

YOU'LL GET US ALL IN TROUBLE!!

THWAK THWAK!

HUH!?

HUH!?

CON-SIDER THE DANGER, YOU FOOL!!

NOW THE REAL PLAYERS APPEAR.

GRRR...

QUESTION CORNER
SBS

Q: This is Timmy Ueda of the SBS Takeover Gang!
I'm going to begin the SBS Question Corner before you do,
Oda Sensei!!
SBS will now begin!!

A: Agh! Oh no, you did it!
Darn you, Timmy.
Now I can't do it! Well, I guess it's already begun.

Q: Hello, Oda Sensei. On page 92 of volume 8, in panel
6, it says "Find Panda Man," but I can't find him.
Where is he?

A: Oh, that. I got a lot of postcards
about that. Some people found
him and some didn't. First of all,
I didn't even expect people to
notice those tiny words.
Nevertheless, I'll give the answer.
Inside the lower circle, it does
indeed say, "Find Panda Man!!!" And
Panda Man can be seen in the
circle at the upper right.

THANKS FOR THE BOAT. CAN WE KEEP IT?

KREEK...!!

SEE YOU AROUND.

WE'LL SINK!!

WE'LL SINK!!

(THE SCENE IN QUESTION)

← Close-up, lower left

Close-up, upper right →

→ He's making a peace sign.

Chapter 83:
LUFFY IN BLACK

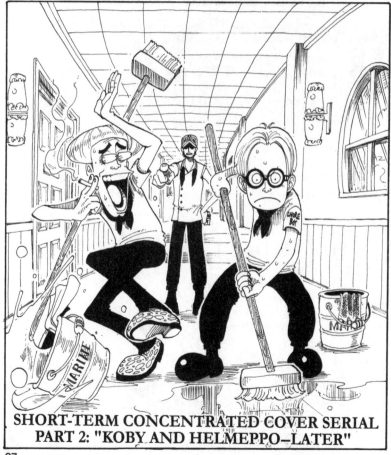

SHORT-TERM CONCENTRATED COVER SERIAL PART 2: "KOBY AND HELMEPPO–LATER"

OOOOOO...

LET'S SEE WHAT THESE GUYS CAN DO.

VEEN

klik klik klik...

A HUMAN WHO'S A MATCH FOR THE FISH-MEN.

DA-DOOM!!

WE SHOULD'VE CRUSHED THESE HUMANS AS SOON AS THEY SHOWED UP!

...YOU'LL DESTROY ARLONG PARK!!

SMEK. ♥

IF YOU LOSE YOUR TEMPER...

......

LORD ARLONG, PLEASE DON'T GET WORKED UP.

YEAH!!

THERE'S A LITTLE PROBLEM, GUYS...

OCTOPUS SHOULD BE BOILED IN SALT WATER, SLICED, AND SEASONED WITH OLIVE OIL AND PAPRIKA. IT'S GREAT WITH BOOZE.

THAT OCTOPUS IS UP TO SOMETHING.

TIME FOR...

ZERO VISIBILITY.

DOOM

FLOOSH

!!

HACHI INK JET!!!

KA-BOOSH!!!

I'VE ENTERED THE FRAY ON BEHALF OF THAT FOOL OF A CAPTAIN.

HOORAY, SANJI!!

WHAT HAVE I DONE?

KLAK.

KLAK. KLAK...

...HE'S NOT SO BAD!!

BUT HEY, COMPARED TO A BUNCH OF WOMAN-HATING CRAP-PIRATES...

KLUNK!!

HE'S INCREDIBLE!!

YOU SAID IT...

STILL?

MY FEET STILL WON'T COME OUT!

HUH?

...BUT THAT WAS A RATHER GALLANT ACT FOR A PIRATE.

YOU'RE PRETTY STRONG, FOR A HUMAN...

...TO TAKE ME ON, HUMAN.

I DON'T THINK YOU'VE GOT WHAT IT TAKES...

I WAS RAISED BY A PIRATE.

WANNA TEST MY GALLANTRY, CRAP-FISH?

NOPE. NOT YET.

HOW 'BOUT NOW?

I DUNNO, I THINK THEY'RE JUST STRETCHING.

THEN HOW 'BOUT HELPING ME!?

HOW ABOUT NOW, LUFFY!?

YOU'RE AT ARLONG PARK!!!

YOU THINK THIS IS FUN AND GAMES, FOOLS!?

WAAAAH!!!

WHOOM

I'LL SMASH YOU!!!

C'MON, LUFFY! TRY POINTING YOUR TOES!!

TMP TMP TMP TMP TMP

!?

HEY, OCTO-PUS.

THEY'RE BUSY RIGHT NOW.

KREK

KREK...!!

I ALMOST FORGOT ABOUT YOU!!

GRRR!!

RORONOA ZOLO!!

WHY DON'T YOU SMASH ME?

YOU MUST REALLY WANT ME TO HURT YOU!!

AAAAAAAH!!!

WAAAAAAH!!!

TMP

TMP TMP TMP

SHOOM!!!

BROTHER USOPP!!

...!!

JUDGING FROM THE WEAPONS YOU'RE HOLDING...

AND THAT MEANS THAT EVERY ONE OF YOU HAS TO...

...I'D SAY THIS IS A REBELLION.

YOU'RE FROM COCO VILLAGE, AREN'T YOU?

SMEK. ♥

HEY, DIDN'T YOU GUYS COME HERE TO CHALLENGE US?

YOU'RE STILL HERE?

HE'S ONE OF THE PIRATES TOO?

ISN'T HE THE GUY THAT SAVED GENZO AT THE VILLAGE?

WAP!!

DO YOU FOOLS ACTUALLY THINK YOU CAN BEAT US?

...SOMETHING YOU WANT TO SAY?

IS THERE...

NOW LET GO OF MY HAND!!

DARN RIGHT WE DO!!

YEAH, WE ACTUALLY DO.

KRAK
KRAK
KRAK

!?

WHAM!!

NO...NO THANKS!!

OF COURSE, IN YOUR CONDITION, YOU'D SINK ANYWAY!!

PEOPLE WHO'VE EATEN THE DEVIL FRUIT CAN'T SWIM.

HEY! PUT ME DOWN!!

I KNOW A GAME WE CAN PLAY.

HA HA HA HA HA!!

WOOOOO.O!!

...PISTOL!!!!

...OCEAN!!

NOT THE...

GUM-GUM...

UNH...

KRK!!

EXCELLENT PLAN.

FINISH THESE CUSTOMERS OFF, THEN DRAG HIM OUT?

THERE'S ONLY ONE WAY TO RESCUE LUFFY!!

JUMPING INTO THE OCEAN IS JUST WHAT THEY WANT US TO DO!!!

HA HA HA HA HA!!

TIME TO PLAY, EH?

YEAH!!!

LET'S DO IT!!!

KLAKLANK!!

WOOOOOO

TMPTMPTMP!!

AAAAAH!!

GLUB GLUB

THIS IS BAD. I HAVE NO STRENGTH...

Q: When Arlong and the other Fish-Men have children, do they lay eggs like fish do?

A: (Buzz) The Fish-Men are actually mammals, so they have kids the same way humans do. Of course, that's the job of the Fish-Women

Q: I, like, totally wanna know the heights of the crew. That Nami is, like, soooo cute!

A: The main five, eh? All right. Um, first of all, Gaimon's height is... Just kidding. Okay, I'll start with the shortest. Nami's 5' 6½", Luffy is 5' 8," Usopp is 5' 8½", Sanji is a little under 5' 10," and Zolo is 5' 10." So basically, they're all like about the same height.

Q: Of the Fish-Men, Hatchan is the cutest and funniest. So what I wonder is, how come his full name is Hatchan and his nickname is Hachi? (In Japanese, "-chan" is usually part of a nickname.)

A: You know how Chinese people sometimes have Chan as a last name? It's kind of the same thing.

Q: What is that thing wrapped around the waists of Usopp and most of the pirates that appear in *One Piece*? A towel? Or are they trying to copy Zolo's haramaki?

A: ⬅ You mean this? Yeah, they're all wearing it, huh. But there's no deep significance to it. It's just a sash. It seems that pirates liked to wear them. But they used to stick pistols and knives in them, so they aren't just for show.

Chapter 84:
ZOMBIE

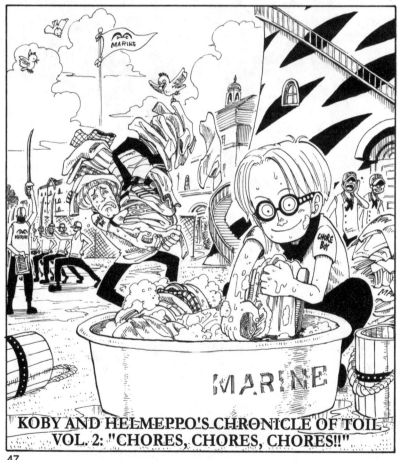

KOBY AND HELMEPPO'S CHRONICLE OF TOIL
VOL. 2: "CHORES, CHORES, CHORES!!"

SH WU

!!!?

SWOOSH—

EEK !!! MY HAIR !!!

HMPH.

UM... THANKS?

...YOU'RE ABSOLUTELY RIGHT!!! HEY, IT'S ONLY HAIR! IT'LL GROW BACK!!

GR

IF YOU THINK I'LL LET YOU GET AWAY WITH THAT...

HUMAN SCUM !!!

UH-OH...

.....

WHEEZE

HUFF...!!

WHOOSH !!!

HAH !!!

STAY ON YOUR TOES IF YOU WANT TO LIVE A WHILE LONGER !!

TH

SWAK!!

WELL, A FISH SHOULD NEVER PIT HIMSELF AGAINST A COOK !!!

OH, YEAH !?

THE PAIN!! MY LUNGS ARE BURSTING!!

GLUB

GLUB

...!!

TUM———...P!!

NOW DO YOU GET IT!?

SEE, RORONOA ZOLO!? I'M MORE THAN A MATCH FOR ANY SWORDSMAN.

VMMMBB...B

FWASH!!

WHO OM!

'''SWORD CATCH!!!

HACHI'S TRIPLE...

YEAH, YOU TALK A LOT !!!

I HEARD YOU USE A THREE-SWORD STYLE.

STOP STALLING!!!

WHAT THE HECK!? GET DOWN HERE!!!

SO WHY ONLY ONE SWORD!?

...

SHUT UP!! I'M NOT EVEN TRYING!!!

YOU'RE LOSING PLENTY AGAINST JUST ONE SWORD, FISH!!

GLUB

GLUB

...A HUMAN SWORDSMAN CAN NEVER BEAT ME!!!

THERE'S A REASON WHY...

WE'VE GOT TO DO SOMETHING TO SAVE HIM!!

BUT AT THIS RATE, BROTHER LUFFY'S DOOMED!!

BUT IF WE DIVE INTO THE OCEAN NOW, THEY'LL JUST DRAG US TO THE BOTTOM!!

DARN!! THAT SLIPPERY OCTOPUS CLOWN IS WASTING OUR PRECIOUS TIME!!

MR. GENZO...

I'LL GO HELP THAT YOUNG RUBBER BOY.

YOU THINK YOU CAN ACCOMPLISH ANYTHING IN THE OCEAN, INJURED LIKE YOU ARE!?

BUT...

KLIK

KLIK...

THROB

THROB

OUCH!!!

WAIT FOR US!!

TUP!

ZING!!

AND ME!!

COUNT ME IN!

ME TOO, MR. GENZO.

I'LL GO, TOO!!

BUT, MR. GENZO!

I'LL GO ALONE!!

...AND THE RUBBER BOY AND HIS FRIENDS WILL HAVE FOUGHT FOR NOTHING.

THAT'S AN ORDER.

IF THE FISH-MEN SPOT A CROWD OF US IN THE WATER, THEY'LL ATTACK...

NO!!

IT'S MY LITTLE SISTER THOSE GUYS ARE FIGHTING FOR!

NOJIKO!! BUT YOUR STOMACH...

MR. GENZO, I'M GOING TOO!!

WE'LL LEAVE YOU TO IT! BUT HURRY!

GOOD LUCK!!

RIGHT!!

COME ON!! WE HAVE TO HURRY!!

TMP TMP!!

...!!

WHOOM

...!!

DO YOU KNOW WHY NO HUMAN COULD EVER BEAT ME?

FWUMP...

HUH!?

WHAT!?

KLAK KLANK

FWO OM...!!

HUH!?

?

WH

AH HA HA HA!

AP!!

KA-B L O O SH

HUFF...

HUFF...

AAAAAGH!!!

I'LL CRUSH YOU.

I THOUGHT IT WAS STRANGE THAT HE COULD GET CUT UP LIKE THAT AND RECOVER SO FAST!!

THAT STUPID IDIOT.

OF COURSE! THEY WOULD'VE KILLED ANY NORMAL MAN-- OR AT LEAST CRIPPLED HIM FOR HALF A YEAR!!

OUR BROTHER'S BEEN SUFFERING IN SILENCE ALL THIS TIME!!

SO THOSE WOUNDS WERE TOO DEEP, AFTER ALL...

FWUMP!!

twitch

CRAP...

WHY NOW OF ALL TIMES!?

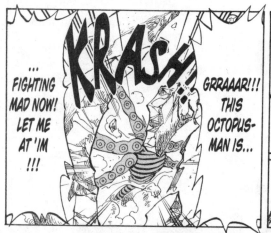

... FIGHTING MAD NOW! LET ME AT 'IM !!!

GRRAAAR!!! THIS OCTOPUS-MAN IS...

HOW LONG ARE YOU GONNA SLEEP!? HACHI!! WAKE UP!!

NO MERE HUMAN COULD EVER BEAT ME, EVEN IF HEAVEN AND EARTH TURNED UPSIDE DOWN !!!

I'M THE SECOND BEST SWORDS-MAN ON FISH-MAN ISLAND!! THEY CALL ME HACHI OF THE SIX-SWORD STYLE!!! DID YOU KNOW THAT!!?

SIX-SWORD STYLE? SOUNDS SILLY.

IS THAT FOR CHOPPING VEGETABLES!?

WHO ARE YOU GOING TO FIGHT, HACHI?

HUH?

HUH!!?

...NO ONE CAN TAKE MY LIFE!!!

LISTEN UP, OCTOPUS!!

THERE'S A MAN I HAVE TO MEET, AND UNTIL I SEE HIM AGAIN...

I'LL KILL YOU, RORONOA ZOLO!!!

HE'S ALIVE, EH?

YEAH, ZOLO!!!

YOSAKU, JOHNNY...YOUR SWORDS!

NOW I'LL SHOW YOU THE THREE-SWORD STYLE.

HMPH. THAT'S IT?

WHID WHID

TUMP!!

GULP...!!

...!!

FWIK

...THEN THOSE KICKS THE CRAP-GEEZER USED TO LAY ON ME MUST'VE BEEN 400TH DEGREE.

DOOM!!

PLIP...

IF THAT WAS A 40TH-DEGREE PUNCH...

TWP TWP

AAAAAAAAAAH!!!

GLUB

GLUB

!

Q: Here goes! Oooone! Twoooo!! Threeeee!!!

A: Thump!!!!

Q: One more time! ♡ Oooone.♡ Twoooo.♡
Threeeee.♡

A: Thump!!! Oh...I'm being played.

Q: Yo! Wassup? ONE PIECE is A-OK! It's always lots of fun and a regular storm of emotions. This is my first time writing to a manga artist. ♡
Oda Sensei, you're a character I like.

A: I'm not a character.

Q: The other day a friend asked me to draw Shanks, so I did. Then suddenly my friend hit me on the head and said, "How come you drew Django!?" Am I sick?

A: Yes. It's an illness. It's "Django Drawer's Disease." You just keep drawing Django. Late-stage symptoms include drawing Django even when you're signing for deliveries, so please be careful.

Q: That thing that's perched on Zeff's head on page 121 of volume 8 is a hat, right? My mom won't believe me. She says, "It's too tall to be a hat. There must be a pole behind him." Sensei, please tell her yourself so the blockhead (age 44) will believe it.

A: Er, Mom, please listen carefully. In this world, there are facts that cannot be bent and realities from which we cannot avert our eyes. The thing that looms above Zeff's head is a "Tower of Faith" that rises up because of his spirit. It is called the "Blue Heavens-Dividing Chef's Hat!' It's true!!!!

Chapter 85:
THREE SWORDS VS. SIX

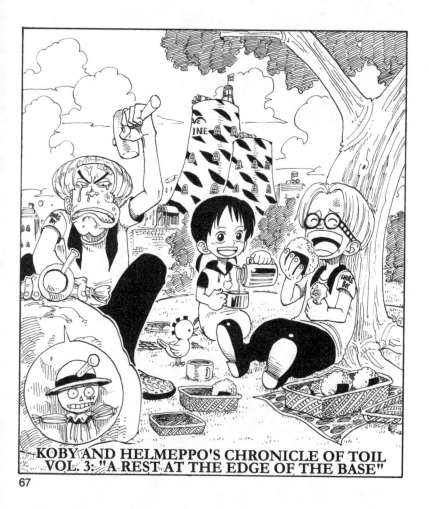

KOBY AND HELMEPPO'S CHRONICLE OF TOIL
VOL. 3: "A REST AT THE EDGE OF THE BASE"

ONLY BROTHER ZOLO CAN CLEAN UP THIS ISLAND!!

BUT THERE'S NO TIME TO WORRY ABOUT THAT.

WHUP!!

IF THOSE WOUNDS OPEN NOW...

...HE'LL DIE FOR SURE...

BROTHER ZOLO'S IN BAD SHAPE!!

HIS WOUNDS HAVE MADE HIM FEVERISH!

DO

OOn.

RORONOA ZOLO, YOU LOOK LIKE A WALKING CORPSE, AND I HAVEN'T EVEN STARTED ON YOU YET.

SWISH

TUN

K...!!

KEEP YOUR COMMENTS TO YOUR-SELF.

FWIP
FWIP

FWIP
FWIP

WHOOSH!!

CATCH, BROTHER!!!

WE THREW THEM TO YOU!! CATCH THEM!!!

FWIP FWIP FWIP FWIP

BROTHER!! OUR SWORDS!!

THIS IS BAD... I'M ABOUT TO PASS OUT. AND MY FEVER, INSTEAD OF GOING DOWN, IS RISING!!

HUFF... HUFF...

BROTHER ZOLO, LOOK OUT!!!

FWIP FWIP

FWIP FWIP

wobble wobble

THIS IS THE SIX-SWORD STYLE, WHICH CAN ONLY BE PERFORMED BY SOMEONE WITH SIX ARMS AND A CHARMINGLY FLEXIBLE BODY.

I'LL SHOW YOU A WORLD THAT NO TWO-ARMED HUMAN CAN ENTER!!!

JUST THINK ABOUT IT MATHEMATICALLY. THREE BLADES...

...IS THE MAXIMUM YOU CAN HOLD. YOU HAVE NO CHANCE AGAINST MY SIX BLADES.

I'M GOING TO CHOP YOU UP!!!

WHY DO YOU FIGHT SO HARD WHEN YOU CANNOT WIN?

WHAT DRIVES YOU?

THAT WOULD BE A GRAVE MISCALCULATION.

MATHEMATICALLY!?

THEY'RE MUCH WEIGHTIER THAN YOURS ARE!!!

I MAY ONLY HAVE THREE BLADES, BUT LOOK AT THEM!

WOₒₒₒₒOₒOₒ

DARN IT! I DON'T KNOW IF THIS WILL WORK ON THE OCEAN FLOOR!!!

KLANG

GLUG

HE'S SWALLOWED AN AWFUL LOT OF WATER!! IF WE CAN'T FREE HIM SOON, IT'LL BE TOO LATE!!

GLUG

GLUG

THE WATER'S BUOYANCY IS TOO STRONG!!

KLANG

KLANG!!

GLUG

GLUG

I NEED AN OXYGEN TANK, BUT THERE'S NO TIME TO GET ONE!!

AND I CAN'T CARRY HIM TO THE SURFACE WITH THE THING ATTACHED!!

IT'S NO USE! I CAN'T BREAK THE ROCK!!!

HURRY!

MR. GENZO...

THAT'S IT!!

GLUG

74

AND HE EVEN MANAGED TO CUT UP MY HANDS!

THAT HUMAN MATCHED THE ROTATION OF MY BLADES AND PASSED RIGHT BETWEEN THEM!

WELL I'M A SWORDSMAN, NOT AN ACROBAT!!!

YOSAKU, ALL THIS FIGHTING'S SURE TO OPEN UP BROTHER ZOLO'S WOUNDS!!

WHAT COULDA HAPPENED!!?

HOW!?

HUH!!?

THWUMP...

BROTHER ZOLO LOOKS LIKE HE'S IN PAIN!!

I'D TRADE PLACES WITH HIM IF I COULD.

HUFF

HUFF

OH, NOW I'VE REALLY HAD IT WITH YOU! I'M REALLY GONNA KILL YOU!!!

plup plup...

KLAN---G

KLAN---G!!

...OCTOPUS POT STANCE!!! YOU'RE AS GOOD AS DEAD!!!

SIX-SWORD STYLE...

...I CANNOT FALL.

EVEN IF MOST PEOPLE WOULD PASS OUT FROM WOUNDS LIKE THESE...

plup plup

FWOOSH!!!

THIS TECHNIQUE IS 100% UNSTOPPABLE!!!

IT ALREADY WORKED ON YOU ONCE!!!

...I CANNOT DIE.

EVEN IF THESE WOUNDS WOULD KILL MOST PEOPLE...

WHEEZE

KLA-KL

NEW YEAR'S...

--GIRI!!!

BANG!!!

I CANNOT FALL.

I HAVE TO LIVE TO DEFEAT "HAWK-EYE" MIHAWK.

SW up...

ONI--

SRIK

SRIK...

HUH...?

EH, OCTOPUS BOY!? ARE YOU SATISFIED!?

NOW DO YOU SEE WHOSE SWORDS ARE WEIGHTIER?

DRAGON...

HE
COULDN'T
HAVE...

HACHI
...

HOW...
COULD I
LOSE TO
ONLY
THREE
SWORDS
?

WHA-KRASH!!

KLAK

I HAVE
TO SAVE
LUFFY!!

THE
REST O
YOU AR
BENEAT
MY
NOTICE

RORONOA ZOLO!! HOW DARE YOU DO THAT TO HACHI!!?

RRM MM BBB

HMPH... I NEVER THOUGHT THERE WAS A HUMAN IN THE EAST BLUE WHO COULD TAKE THE FULL FORCE OF MY PUNCH AND LIVE.

BROTHER COOK...

YOU SENT ME FLYING QUITE A WAYS BEFORE...

DOOM!!

YOU UNDER-ESTIMATE ME.

ESPECIALLY AT A CERTAIN RESTAURANT I KNOW.

DOOM!!

AW, I'LL WAGER THERE ARE LOTS WHO COULD DO IT.

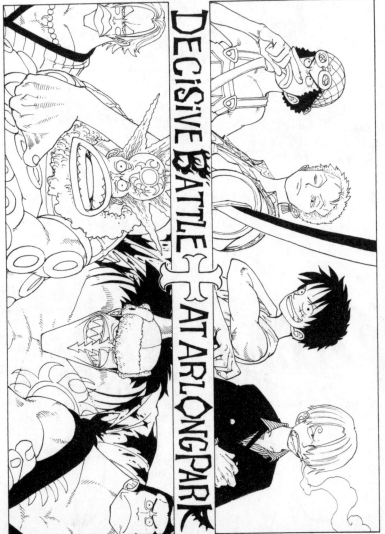

Chapter 86:
HEROISM VS.
FISH-MAN CRUELTY

STOP, ZOLO!!

IF YOU GO INTO THE OCEAN LIKE THAT YOU'LL DIE!!

! WHUP···!!!

HAVE TO HURRY... LUFFY...

I CAN'T WAIT AROUND FOR YOU TO FIGHT!!

I KNOW!!

SHUT UP!! LUFFY'S GOT TO BE AT HIS LIMIT BY NOW!!

!?

I'M STOPPING YOU BECAUSE I KNOW THAT ALL TOO WELL, CRAP-SWORDSMAN!!

I KNOW THERE'S NO TIME.

WHAT!? ISN'T THAT...

...THE VILLAGE HEADMAN !!?

!?

DO

Om!!

GLUB

GLUB

IS THAT LUFFY'S STRETCHED NECK!?

HURRY, BEFORE MY BREATH RUNS OUT...

WUMP

WUMP

PLEASE LET US BE IN TIME!!!

C'MON, BREATHE!!

WHUMP

WHUMP

...WITH THIS STRETCHY NECK OF YOURS, YOU COULD AT LEAST COUGH UP WATER AND BREATHE!!

I'M SORRY!! I DON'T HAVE THE STRENGTH TO BRING UP YOUR WHOLE BODY, BUT...

THAT'S IT, MR. GENZO!!

YES!!

PHOOSH

WHUMP

WHUMP

...AND LEAVE THE REST TO THE OLD MAN!!

GLUB GLUB

THEN I JUST HAVE TO SHATTER THE ROCK WITH A KICK...

GLUB

GLUB

GOOD. NOW EVEN WITH HIS FEET IN THE ROCK, HE CAN AT LEAST BREATHE!!

FISH-MAN KARATE ...

FOREARM SLEDGE !!!

!!?

HMPH, IT'S THOSE WORMS FROM COCO VILLAGE! BUT THEY'RE WASTING THEIR TIME !!

BLOOP BLOOP!!

...!!!

!!?

I'LL DROWN YOU RIGHT NOW !!!

GLUB GLUB GLUB

DO YOU REALLY THINK YOUR EFFORTS...

...WILL BUY YOU ANY MORE TIME IN THIS WORLD !?

I'VE BEEN SPOTTED BY A FISH-MAN!!

GLUB

OH NO !!

GLUB

THWAP!!

NOT IF I CAN HELP IT!!

IT'LL BE ALL YOU CAN DO JUST TO HOLD YOUR BREATH, HUMAN!!

YOU WANT TO FIGHT *ME* UNDERWATER!?

...!!

WHAP!!

⁉

THE DUELLING HAIR TETHER!!!

ALL RIGHT, THEN. I'LL TAKE YOU ON!!

HMPH. THAT WAS WEAK. DOWN HERE YOUR KICKS HAVE HALF THE FORCE THEY'D HAVE ON LAND.

BUT WITH FISH-MAN KARATE, THERE'S NO LOSS OF POWER IN THE WATER.

SHUP...

BLOOSHH

BOWEL-BUSTER!!!

INSTANT UNDER-SEA...

IN FACT, THE POWER OF SOME MOVES IS EVEN MULTIPLIED!!

GLUB

GLUB

GLUB

FWRRR RRR

GLUB

FLAMING AXE KICK !!!

GLUB !!

KRAK!!

BACK FOOT JAW-BREAKER !!!

UNGH!! I LET OUT TOO MUCH AIR!! I NEED AIR! AIR!!

WHERE ARE *YOU* GOING?

PLOOF !!!

YOUR ABILITY TO TAKE PUNISHMENT IS ANNOYING. IT'S NOT NORMAL FOR A HUMAN.

CRAP!!! LET ME PASS!!! AIR!!! I GOTTA BREATHE !!!

YOU WANT TO ESCAPE FROM ME, BUT YOU CAN'T.

GLUB

THIS GAME ENDS IN ONLY ONE WAY... DEATH.

GLUB

BUT LET ME EXPLAIN TO YOU THE CONSEQUENCES OF YOUR FOOLHARDY HEROISM!!!

!!

THEN I'LL FINISH OFF THAT LONG-NOSED FOOL AND ZOLO, AND I'LL KILL ALL THE VILLAGERS FOR THEIR REBELLION!!

THE RUBBER MAN WILL DIE AT THE SAME TIME.

....!!

AND WHEN YOU'RE FINISHED, I'LL KILL THE VILLAGE HEADMAN.

IN THE END, YOUR HEROISM IS JUST SO MUCH HOT AIR.

TREMBLE...

AND AFTER ALL THIS, I CAN'T VERY WELL LET THAT TRAITOR NAMI GET AWAY, CAN I !!?

IT CAN'T SAVE A SINGLE SOUL!!!

!!!!

DO YOU UNDER-STAND?

...YOUR GUTS WOULD BE SQUEEZED OUT OF YOUR BODY!!!

IF YOU WERE TO DESCEND RAPIDLY TO THE BOTTOM OF THE OCEAN...

SHWAP...!!

YOU CAN'T EVEN ENDURE EXTREME CHANGES IN WATER PRESSURE!!

YOU HUMANS TRULY ARE POWERLESS CREATURES.

THE OLD MAN WILL HAVE TO TAKE CARE OF LUFFY FOR NOW.

GOTTA CHANGE THE PLAN!!

WOOS

PULVERIZING PRESSURE PLUNGE!!!

CRUKK

AH HA HA HA HA !!!

HE THINKS I CAN'T SAVE ANYONE !?

I WON'T LET HIM GET AWAY WITH THIS!!!

AND WHAT HAPPENED TO SISTER NAMI'S SISTER AND THAT MAN!?

BROTHER COOK'S NOT COMING UP!

THIS FOOL'S STILL NOT DEAD!?

...BREATHE WITH THEIR LUNGS ON LAND AND SWITCH TO GILLS IN THE WATER!! SO RIGHT NOW, HE'S JUST A TALKING FISH!!

THESE FISH-MEN...

ALL RIGHT THEN, WE'LL DO IT AGAIN !!!

FWOM!!

FISH DIE WHEN AIR IS FORCED THROUGH THEIR GILLS!!

FWOOO!!

WE'RE NEAR THE SURFACE NOW. THINK YOU CAN SURVIVE A SECOND PLUNGE?

AND IT SHOULD BE THE SAME WITH HIM !!!

FWOOOOO

GWAAAGH !!!!

I'M MANY TIMES STRONGER THAN YOU ARE. IT DOESN'T MATTER IF WE'RE IN WATER OR OUT OF IT.

KOFF!! YOU STILL DON'T UNDERSTAND.

KOFF!!

AND NOW YOU'VE MADE ME MAD.

SPLASHHH...!!

BUT MY GREATEST MOVE IS THE THOUSAND-BRICK FIST. THE LIKELIHOOD OF YOUR SURVIVAL IS...ZERO!!!

I SENT YOU FLYING BEFORE WITH THE HUNDRED-BRICK FIST.

WO WO

I'LL DESTROY YOU WITH THE ULTIMATE MOVE OF FISH-MAN KARATE.

WHAM!!!

COLLIER* COUP !!!

!

*COLLIER IS THE FRENCH TERM FOR "NECK MEAT."

*ÉPAULE = SHOULDER. (NOTE: THE ASTERISKS ON THIS PAGE INDICATE FRENCH WORDS.)

*SELLE = SADDLE (AS IN "SADDLE OF MUTTON")

*CÔTELETTE = BACK

*GIGOT = THIGH

*POITRINE = BREAST MEAT

*MOUTON = LAMB

Chapter 87:
IT'S ALL OVER!!

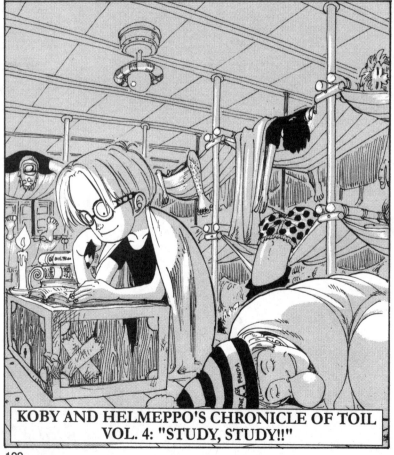

KOBY AND HELMEPPO'S CHRONICLE OF TOIL VOL. 4: "STUDY, STUDY!!"

KA-BLOOSH!!

WOOOOOO OO OOOO O

OOO OO

HACHI ...

KUROOBI ...

LOOKS LIKE WE'RE THE WINNERS OF THIS GAME.

LIKE I SAID, INSIGNIFICANT SMALL FRY.

HOW DARE YOU WIPE OUT MY MOST VALUABLE OFFICERS !?

WHO DO YOU THINK YOU ARE !!!?

I'LL HAVE TO GO BACK DOWN TO THE OCEAN FLOOR.

IT MEANS HE'S NOT DEAD... YET.

WHAT'S THAT MEAN?

YOU SAID LUFFY'S HALF-OKAY.

WHEEZE WHEEZE

KLAK

...THAT GUY ISN'T ABOUT TO LET ME.

BUT IT LOOKS LIKE...

THOSE GUYS ARE INCREDIBLE! THEY DEFEATED TWO OF ARLONG'S BEST MEN!!

.....!!

HE'S COUGHING UP WATER. WE'RE SO CLOSE!

TAKE A BREAK, MR. GENZO!! I'LL GO DOWN NOW!!

HAAAH!! HAAAH!! THAT'S IT! I CAN'T HOLD MY BREATH ANY LONGER!!

huff

huff

GASP!

SPLASH!!

I STILL CAN HARDLY BELIEVE IT, BUT ...

I WAS AFRAID TO BELIEVE IT UNTIL NOW.

NOBODY'S BEEN KILLED, YET!! IN FACT...

HOW'S IT GOING OVER THERE!?

huff

huff

...ABOUT THIS BATTLE!!!

I FEEL A RISING SENSE OF HOPE...

DOOM!!

AND YOU WERE PRETTY FAST, FOR A HUMAN!!

BUT THEN YOU DIED FROM ONE SHOT OF MY LIP-O-BLASTER. HOW DISAPPOINTING.

DOOM!!

SMEK! ♡ YOU GAVE ME A HARD CHASE.

MY COMRADES SHOULD BE FINISHED BY NOW TOO.

TMP
TMP

GUESS I'LL HEAD BACK...

THAT GUY THINKS HE HIT ME WITH HIS *LIP-O-BLISTER* THING!! HEE HEE...JUST KEEP WALKING, LIPS!!

plip...

SUCCESS!! I'M SAVED!! GOOD THING I MADE THOSE KETCHUP STARS FOR JUST THIS KIND OF SITUATION !!

TMP
TMP

BA-BUMP
BLINK
BA-BUMP
BA-BUMP

I DO FEEL SORRY FOR NAMI...

...AND I WISH I COULD DO MORE TO HELP, BUT IF IT MEANS GETTING KILLED, I'LL PASS.

SHEESH, BUT WHAT A TERRIFYING SPECIES THEY ARE.

THEY CAN FLIP HOUSES UPSIDE DOWN! A WHOLE VILLAGE OF 'EM!!

tmp   tmp

...THEN I MIGHT LOOK LIKE I FOUGHT A REAL BATTLE!

THAT'S IT! IF I SMEAR DIRT ALL OVER MYSELF...

WHAT SHOULD I SAY WHEN I GET BACK?

RUB RUB

...I WISH I HAD...A FEW MORE BATTLE SCARS!!

I'M COVERED WITH KETCHUP BLOOD, BUT...

UMM, DON'T CRY, NAMI. IT WAS A HOPELESS BATTLE.

UMM, I ALMOST HAD HIM, BUT HE GOT AWAY.

RUB RUB

WE'RE A TEAM, AREN'T WE?

UMM, SORRY. I LOST.

RUB

IT'S BUSINESS. I HAD NO CHOICE.

BUT HEY, COMPARED TO A BUNCH OF WOMAN-HATING CRAP PIRATES, HE'S NOT SO BAD!!

UMM, WOW, THAT WAS ONE TOUGH FIGHT!

UMM, WELL, WE ALL PUT UP A GOOD FIGHT.

I PREFER DEATH TO DEFEAT.

116

CAN YOU UNDERSTAND WHAT A PAINFUL CHOICE THAT WAS FOR HER?

WE'VE BEEN WAITING FOR YOU, BROTHERS!!!

UMM, MY WOUNDS AREN'T THAT BAD!!

......!!

RUB...

RUB...

......

RUB*

RUB...

RUB...!!

UMM, YOU SHOULDA SEEN ME FIGHT...

LET'S FIGHT!!!

THIS IS SHAMEFUL!!!!

SWIP

SHAKE

SHAKE

SHAKE

TOMP

LUFFY AND THOSE GUYS LIVE EVERY DAY LIKE THERE'S NO TOMORROW!!

YOU THINK I'D LET YOU HIT ME WITH YOUR WIMPY HALF-FISH SQUIRT GUN!!?

THE MOMENT I DECIDED TO LEAVE MY VILLAGE, I SAID GOODBYE TO PEACE AND SECURITY!!

SHAKE
SHAKE
SHAKE

BECAUSE I WANTED TO LAUGH WITH GUSTO, LIKE THEM !!!

ERK.... !

THAT'S THE REASON I SET OUT TO SEA IN THE FIRST PLACE!!

THAT'S WHY THEY CAN LAUGH SO HEARTILY!!

KREEEK!!

HOW COULD I EVER LAUGH WITH THEM !!?

DEATH BLOW !!

IF I DON'T FIGHT WITH EVERYTHING I'VE GOT...

...THEN I'M NOT WORTHY TO SAIL ON THE SAME SHIP WITH THOSE GUYS!!!

FW UMP...!!

YOUR BRAIN MUST BE AS WEAK AS YOUR BODY.

SMEK.♡

YOU SHOULD'VE JUST PLAYED DEAD.

PLIP

PLIP.

THWAK

THWAK

UNGH!!

AGH!

THWAK-THWAK!!! THWAK

THAT'S RIGHT. IT'S ALL OVER FOR YOU !!!

IT'S ALL OVER.

twitch

twitch

THE LITTLE COWARD.

BA-DOOM!!!

GRAAAAH!!

WHAT!!? THE FOOL TRICKED ME!!

HE RAN AWAY !!

WHAP...!!

BOOZE !?

FURRR R !!

BLOOSH!!

SPURT

SHUNK!!

UGH !!!

THE DEADLY LEAD STAR !!!

SPURT

...I'LL BLAST YOU WITH THE WATER FROM THIS PADDY!!!

SMEK·♡

SHLURRG

BUT NO MATTER WHERE YOU'RE HIDING...

GRR!! THIS PUNY HUMAN IS FULL OF INSOLENT TRICKS!!

WH'UP...!!

P·L·P...

SMEK. ♡

I'M A PIRATE NOW!!

IF I LOSE, I DIE!!

huff...

WHATEVER HAPPENS, I, USOPP, WILL NOT RUN FROM THIS FIGHT!!!

THAT FISH CAN SAY WHATEVER HE WANTS!

BOOM!!

LIP-O-CANNON!!!!

KA-BLOOSH!!!

KRAK KRAK KREK KREK`·· !!!

THWUMP!

WOW !!!

WHAT POWER !!!

DO——OM

SCARY

THERE HE IS.

WHY DO I HAVE TO FIGHT *THIS* FOOL?

!!

Q: Sensei! I thought up a new technique for Luffy. He stretches his mouth and eats up his enemy and later flushes him down the toilet along with his *oop! What do you think? Good idea, huh?

A: It stinks-o.

Q: I've got a question for Oda Sensei. Whaddaya call Belle-Mère's hairdo?

A: It's called "women are brave." Go to the beauty parlor and shout it out.

Q: I'm glad that brother Sanji is a ladies' man and not a "gentlemen's man."

A: Indeed.

Q: When Sanji is thinking about a girl, his cigarette smoke forms the shape of a heart. How does he do that? I want to do that too!! Please (x100) teach me!

A: Hmm. First you have to be over 20 years old. Then light a cigarette and take a deep puff of smoke. Let the smoke soak up the feelings of love that you've prepared in your lungs and exhale it from your mouth. The smoke will surely come out in the shape of a heart.

Q: I can't quite decide whether Yosaku and Johnny are strong or not. I'm within a frog's hair of being able to tell. But really, between those two and Helmeppo, who will develop more?

A: I have high hopes that, one day, Kaya will become an excellent doctor.

Chapter 88:
DIE!!!

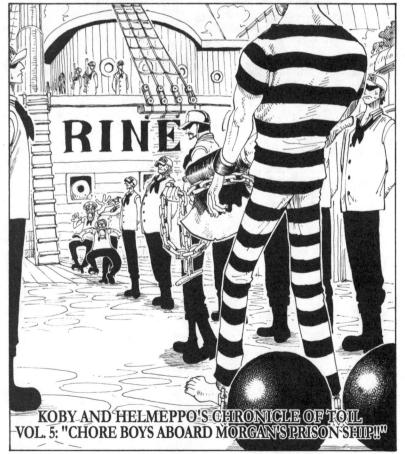

**KOBY AND HELMEPPO'S CHRONICLE OF TOIL
VOL. 5: "CHORE BOYS ABOARD MORGAN'S PRISON SHIP!!"**

HAMMER
!!!!

SP LA——SH!!

SSSSSS——SS!!

USOPP'S HAMMER!!

USOPP'S RUBBER BAND OF DOOM!!!

USOPP'S HAMMER!

USOPP'S HAMMER!

USOPP'S HAMMER!

!!!!?

WHY... YOU...

TWITCH!!

I'VE DONE MY CRYING !!

AND I'VE VOICED MY COMPLAINTS !!

KRK

UNH !!

MY MIND IS MADE UP!!

TMP TMP TMP TMP TMP...

I HAVE TO GO ...

...AND JOIN THE FIGHT!!!

...BUT THEN THEY COUGHED UP BLOOD AND COLLAPSED!!

I DON'T KNOW. IT LOOKED LIKE HE JUST SPLASHED THEM WITH WATER...

WHOA... WHAT DID THAT NASTY SHARK DO?

WAS IT ALL A DREAM!?

GLUB GLUB ...!!

WHUMP

WHUMP

BREATHE !!

PLEASE ...

SPLUP!!

WHAT'S HAPPENED TO BROTHER LUFFY!? HE COULDN'T HAVE DIED, COULD HE?

BROTHER COOK!! STAY DOWN!!

DID HE MOVE !?

JUST A LITTLE MORE !!!

TWITCH

ACK!!

COME BACK TO LIFE!! PLEASE!!!

.....

WHUMP!

.....!!!

WHUMP!!!

WHUMP

STAGGER....!!

.....

BUT HE'S LIKE A SHOTGUN BLAST!!! SO THIS IS THE POWER OF A SHARK...EVEN AMONG THE FISH-MEN, HE'S IN A CLASS BY HIMSELF!!

THIS GUY'S... NO JOKE!! HE MAKES IT LOOK EASY.

KOFF!!

ACK!!!

YOUR LIVES ARE WORTH-LESS.

GO AHEAD AND DIE.

THIS IS LIKE NOTHING WE'VE FACED SO FAR!!

DO ZOM!!

ARLONG !!!!

NAMI ...

SISTER NAMI !!

WHAT BRINGS YOU HERE?

I WAS JUST ABOUT TO BLAST THIS NO-ACCOUNT PIRATE TO BITS.

MISS NAMI... ♡

NAMI ...

...TO KILL YOU !!!

I'VE COME ...

I'D PREFER THAT YOU KEEP WORKING FOR ME OF YOUR OWN FREE WILL.

BUT I'M A REASONABLE FISH-MAN!

I DON'T WANT TO HOLD A YOUNG GIRL AGAINST HER WILL.

...IF YOU'RE WILLING TO REJOIN MY CREW...

...AND AGREE TO BE AN OFFICER AND DRAW OCEAN CHARTS...

...EXCEPT FOR YOU. HOWEVER...

NOW, I'M ABOUT TO KILL EVERY HUMAN HERE...

THEY'VE CAUSED ME TOO MUCH TROUBLE.

BUT THESE TWO DIE, OF COURSE.

...I'M WILLING TO SPARE THE PEOPLE OF COCO VILLAGE.

WHAK!

SO WHAT'S IT GONNA BE?

UNH...

...YOU CAN SEE WHAT A TRAGIC MISTAKE THAT WOULD BE!!

OR STICK WITH THESE WEAKLINGS AND TRY TO FIGHT ME TOGETHER!!

BUT IF YOU LOOK AT THE SHAPE THESE TWO ARE IN...

COME BACK TO ME NOW AND SAVE YOUR BELOVED VILLAGERS...

GULP....!!

ARE YOU MY SHIP-MATE...

WELL, NAMI!!?

...OR THEIRS?

IF I SAY I'M LUFFY AND ZOLO'S SHIPMATE, EVERYONE MAY GET KILLED.

BUT IF I SAY I'M ARLONG'S, ALL OF THE VILLAGERS WILL BE SPARED!! IS IT UP TO ME TO DECIDE WHO LIVES AND WHO DIES!!?

I HAVE TO BELIEVE IN THEM!!!

THAT'S DIRTY!! HE'S GONNA KEEP NAMI NO MATTER WHAT SHE DECIDES!!

...!!

BUT...I...

OKAY !!!!

...WITH ME!!!

FIGHT AND DIE...

I'M SORRY, EVERYONE !!!

!?

142

····

DOOM!!

fwup!

ZOLO...

!?

THAT'S PLENTY!!

SPLASH!!

!

THIRTY SECONDS!! I WON'T LAST MORE THAN THAT.

CHOMP

COULD IT BE THAT RUBBER BRAT!!?

ARLONG PARK HAS NO FOUNTAINS!

146

Chapter 89:
TRADE-OFF

IF I CAN JUST KICK THE ROCK AROUND LUFFY'S LEGS TO PIECES, HE CAN SWING INTO ACTION!!!

HE'S THE ONLY ONE LEFT WITH ANY HOPE OF BEATING ARLONG!!!

GLUB GLUB GLUB

IT'S BROTHER COOK!!! I DON'T KNOW WHAT HE'S DOING DOWN THERE, BUT WE'RE ALL COUNTING ON HIM NOW!!!

BROTHER ZOLO!! HOLD FAST!!

SO IF THAT BRAT IS STILL ALIVE, THEN SOMEONE...

...MUST BE HELPING HIM!!!

...BUT THE OCEAN ALSO TAKES AWAY THEIR WILL TO LIVE.

NOT ONLY DO PEOPLE WITH DEVIL-FRUIT POWERS LOSE THEM UNDER-WATER...

HUH!!?

BLINK!!

shake

shake ...

WHOA!! THE OCTOPUS GUY IS GETTING UP!!

WHAT'S HE GONNA DO?

LOOK OVER THERE!!

...!!

WHAT!!?

THWUMP!!

WHAAAT!!?

DOOM!!

DARN!! I THOUGHT A RUBBER BAND WAS COMING AT ME!!!

ba-bump ba-bump

OCTOPUS ...

wheeze wheeze

YOU AIMED AT ARLONG.

HA HA HA HA HA

SEE!? I SCARED HIM!!!

LEAVE THE REST TO ME!!!

FWUP

GLUB

!

GLUB

GET BACK!!! I CAN SHATTER THAT ROCK.

GLUB..!!

A FISH-MAN!

!!

JUST ONE GOOD KICK!!!

WHOOM!!!

DIE!! DIE!!!

HEH HEH...

WHEEZE

EH?

RRMMMBB I'D BETTER...

...FINISH HIM OFF RIGHT NOW!!!

·····

...WOULD'VE KEPT SOME OF THE WOUNDS FROM OPENING UP!!!

LYING STILL...

HUFF HUFF

!

I MEANT OCTOPUS BOY.

I WASN'T TALKING ABOUT ME!!

IS THAT YOUR IDEA OF A JOKE?

YOU'RE PROBABLY RIGHT.

HUH!!!?

I TOLD YOU. THIS IS OUR GAME... AND WE'RE WINNING.

WHAT!?

PLOO

!!!?

GRAAAAR!!!!

THAT WAS CLOSE!!!

KA-BAM!!!!

WHOA. ...!!

blup blup...

IT'S THE RUBBER BOY!!!

PHEW...

●●●●●!!!

LUFFY!!

BROTHER LUFFY!!!

IDIOT !!!

IT'S ABOUT TIME...

THE RUBBER BOY.

UH-
UNH...

GASP

IT DIDN'T WORK!!!

KLAK KLAK KLAK...

NOOOOO

DID YOU... DO SOME-THING?

SHIVER

!!!!?

RRMMMMBB...

I'M GONNA... KILL HIM!!

WUMP

YEP.

JUST WARM-ING UP.

KRAK KRAK

Q: After reading your manga, Sensei, I'm inspired to follow my dream. My dream is to build a big bridge in America.

A: That's nice. A young man with dreams. I like that. All right then, do it. And if anyone gets in your way I'll go and--wearing hard leather boots--stomp on the pinky toe of his foot, so don't worry. Go for it.

Q: Knock, knock, Oda Sensei. Oda-body home!!?

A: Give me a break.

Q: When Patty the Cook says "I'm turniply saucy," what does it mean?

A: "I'm terribly sorry." He tends to make things sound like food. For example, he might say: "He's quite a man. He did lettuce of ham-glazing a-cheese-mints. Peas apple-aud him." But if *you* say things like that, people will probably look at you funny.

Q: A question for you. Is there a bone in Usopp's nose? I've seen it bend so many times. Like *squish*.

A: I've never seen that. Bend...like squish? How absurd...

Whoa!! It does Bend!!!

Here ends SBS!!

Chapter 90:
WHAT CAN YOU DO?

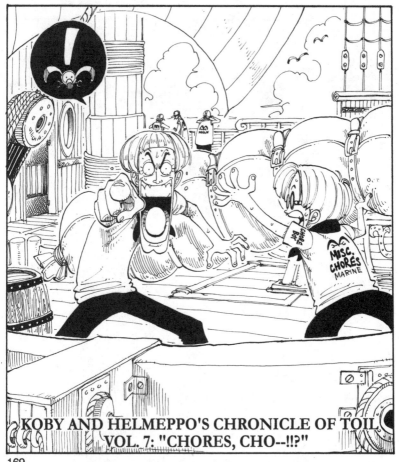

KOBY AND HELMEPPO'S CHRONICLE OF TOIL
VOL. 7: "CHORES, CHO--!!?"

BUT YOU'D HAVE BEEN BETTER OFF DYING PEACEFULLY AT THE BOTTOM OF THE OCEAN.

HA HA HA HA HA... HOW TENACIOUSLY YOU SCUM HOLD ON BY YOUR STUBBY LITTLE TEETH.

UNH!!

UNH!!

WOING WOING

CAN'T YOU UNDER- STAND WHY I'M UPSET?

I'M GLAD THEY RESCUED ME.

UNH!!

I'LL SOON MAKE YOU WISH FOR A QUIET DEATH.

I'VE WATCHED MY BELOVED COMRADES BE DEFEATED BY WORMS!!!

HEY, WHERE DID BROTHER ZOLO FLY OFF TO!?

ALL OF HIS FEROCIOUS ATTACKS DIDN'T EVEN SEEM TO FAZE ARLONG!!

IS BROTHER LUFFY ALL RIGHT?

• • • • •

FWIK

FWIK

FWIK

BIG DEAL.

THWUMP!

GO, LUFFY!! I'VE GOT YOUR BACK!!

KROOSH SPLASH

YOU'RE RIGHT.

THAT WOULD BE THE END OF THE EAST BLUE.

IF LUFFY LOSES, WE'RE ALL DEAD.

WHUP

OUR NOSES.

krok krok

....

DO YOU KNOW THE DIFFERENCE BETWEEN YOU AND ME?

OUR CHINS?

DOOM

WEBBED TOES !!?

I... I THINK HE'S SERIOUS.

IS BROTHER LUFFY JOKING !?

CHOMP!!!

NO- SPECIES !!!!

HUP.

CHONK!! CHONK!! CHONK!! CHONK!!

OOF! UNH! OH! WAH!

GRAAR!!

KRAS...!!!

WAAAAAAH!!! HE CHEWED UP THAT STONE PILLAR!!!

THOOM!!

WOW!! SCARY!

HE'LL BE EATEN UP, BONES AND ALL!!

AAAAA AH

...!?

IF THOSE JAWS CLAMP ONTO LUFFY, THEY WON'T JUST LEAVE MARKS.

FROM THE MOMENT OF BIRTH, AN UNBRIDGEABLE GULF SEPARATES OUR SPECIES !!!

SUPER-HUMAN STRENGTH IS THE BIRTHRIGHT OF ALL FISH-MEN.

YOU'RE INHERENTLY INFERIOR!!!

THE HEAVENS DIDN'T SMILE ON YOUR PUNY KIND IN THAT REGARD.

WHAT'S THIS!? YOU'RE JUST SWINGING WILDLY!!!

I'M BORED WITH YOUR GAMES.

FWOOS

UNH !!!

KLAK KLAK

KLAK...!!!

ENOUGH FOOLISH- NESS.

CLENCH YOUR TEETH !!!

FWRR!!

WHOOSH

WHAT!!?

DOOM!!

GWAAAAH!!!

HE SHATTERED ARLONG'S TEETH!!!!

HUH? WHAT'S HE ON ABOUT?

THOOM

SPLASH!

I DON'T KNOW HOW TO USE A SWORD, SHARK FACE!!!

DOOM!

I DON'T KNOW HOW TO NAVIGATE EITHER!!!

·····

I KNOW I CAN'T LIVE WITHOUT HELP FROM A LOT OF PEOPLE!!!

HEY.

AND I CAN'T TELL LIES!!

FWUP

I CAN'T COOK!!

·····

WHAT A BURDEN IT MUST BE FOR YOUR CREW TO HAVE SUCH AN IDIOT FOR A CAPTAIN.

I DON'T KNOW WHY THEY FIGHT SO DESPERATELY TO SAVE YOU.

BWAH HA HA HA HA HA... WHAT A CLEVER BOY YOU ARE TO ADMIT YOUR OWN HELPLESS-NESS!!!

AN ENDLESS NUMBER OF TIMES!!!

AN ENDLESS NUMBER OF TIMES!!!

KR

KRA

SHEENK

WOW.

THIS IS A SPECIAL POWER BESTOWED BY THE GODS.

.....

CHOMP!!!

...HOW SUPERIOR WE FISH-MEN ARE?

NOW DO YOU SEE...

Luffy's fun idea makes him more than an ideal match for the
toothsome Captain Arlong. During a brief lull in their pitched

You're Reading in the Wrong Direction!!

Whoops! Guess what? You're starting at the wrong end of the comic!

…It's true! In keeping with the original Japanese format, **One Piece** is meant to be read from right to left, starting in the upper-right corner.

Unlike English, which is read from left to right, Japanese is read from right to left, meaning that action, sound effects and word-balloon order are completely reversed… something which can make readers unfamiliar with Japanese feel pretty backwards themselves. For this reason, manga or Japanese comics published in the U.S. in English have sometimes been published "flopped"– that is, printed in exact reverse order, as though seen from the other side of a mirror.

By flopping pages, U.S. publishers can avoid confusing readers, but the compromise is not without its downside. For one thing, a character in a flopped manga series who once wore in the original Japanese version a T-shirt emblazoned with "M A Y" (as in "the merry month of") now wears one which reads "Y A M"! Additionally, many manga creators in Japan are themselves unhappy with the process, as some feel the mirror-imaging of their art skews their original intentions.

We are proud to bring you Eiichiro Oda's **One Piece** in the original unflopped format. For now, though, turn to the other side of the book and let the journey begin…!

–Editor